You Know You're a Minnesotan If...

by
Ed Fischer

Adventure Publications
Cambridge, Minnesota

This book is dedicated to Aaron Vaupel, a Minnesota-nice guy who amazingly prefers to live in Hawaii.

10 9
Text and illustrations, © 1999 by Ed Fischer

Published by Adventure Publications, Inc.
820 Cleveland Street South
Cambridge, MN 55008
1-800-678-7006
www.adventurepublications.net

ISBN-13: 978-1-885061-62-1
ISBN-10: 1-885061-62-5

Minnesota is a special place.

It's 10,000 lakes, Alberta Clippers, Lake Wobegon, Frostbite Falls, fall colors, the fishing opener, the man formerly known as Prince, Jesse Ventura, wild rice pancakes and lutefisk.

It's an Ole and Lena joke, big mosquitos and super steamy saunas where people get sweaty and go out to roll in the snow.

It's home to lots of Scandinavians and Germans, with a spicy mix of Slavs, Italians, Greeks and others who have adopted a Swedish twang and a sense of humor as big as Paul Bunyan.

Minnesotans love to laugh. Mostly, they love to laugh at adversity and at themselves.

You'll see what I mean as you read this book...my view (a loving view) of this bit odd but charming place. As a Minnesotan might say, "It's funnier than a Hoot Owl.'

Search America from sea to sea and you will not find a state that has offered as close a model to the ideal of the successful society as Minnesota.

Neal R. Peirce
The Book of America: Inside 50 States Today

FOOD

You know you're a Minnesotan if...

...you know 101 sneaky ways to get rid of zucchini.

You know you're a Minnesotan if...

...you have a hot dish that can also be used to fix a crack in the ceiling.

You know you're a Minnesotan if...

...you say a casserole is just a hot dish with an attitude.

You know you're a Minnesotan if...

...you were 15 years old before you knew there were other desserts besides jello.

You know you're a Minnesotan if...

...A LITTLE LUNCH: Tomato soup
**   Toasted cheese sandwich**

You know you're a Minnesotan if...

...A FANCY LUNCH: Tomato soup
**   Toasted cheese sandwich**
**   with a pickle**

You know you're a Minnesotan if...

...you go to weddings for the food.

You know you're a Minnesotan if…

…you get high on lutefisk.

You know you're a Minnesotan if…

…you once stood in line at a swedish picnic for 38 minutes to get your free buttered ear of corn.

You know you're a Minnesotan if…

…you gave up lutefisk for Lent.

ED FISCHER

WEATHER

You know you're a Minnesotan if…

...you forget from year to year the procedure you use when you're out of control with your car sliding down the road on ice.

You know you're a Minnesotan if…

...you consider a blizzard a good time to try out your new snow tires even though you have nowhere to go.

You know you're a Minnesotan if…

...you've given some thought to the 5 feet of snow on your roof and that occasional creaking noise.

You know you're a Minnesotan if…

...you feel it's a pretty bad winter if the snow gets higher than the first floor windows.

You know you're a Minnesotan if...

...you stop to ask directions only when it is obvious that death from the elements is imminent.

You know you're a Minnesotan if...

...you love the beauty of newly fallen snow but can only take so much 'beauty.'

You know you're a Minnesotan if...

...you're not sure what you would do if the doors of your car freeze shut while you're in the car.

You know you're a Minnesotan if...

...you have experienced the laughter and hot apple cider on sleigh rides during brisk moonlight nights.

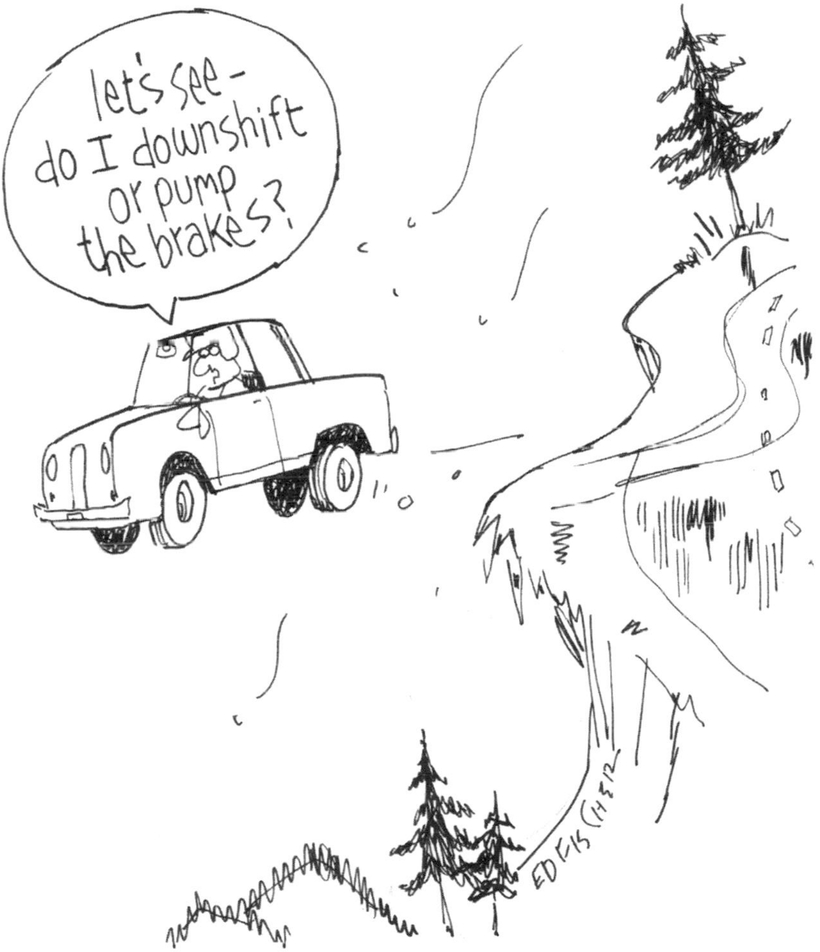
let's see -
do I downshift
or pump
the brakes?
ED FISCHER

You know you're a Minnesotan if...

...you think long underwear is sexy.

You know you're a Minnesotan if...

...you know the only way to get a snow plow to plow your street is to spend two hours shoveling your driveway.

You know you're a Minnesotan if...

...you bought an eight thousand dollar snowmobile so you can go get bread and milk during a blizzard.

You know you're a Minnesotan if...

...you define life in Minnesota as 9 months of winter and 3 months of bad sledding.

Minnesota long underwear in the spring
Louise- do we have any extra strong fabric softener?
ED FISCHER

You know you're a Minnesotan if…

...you feel sex in the winter is a problem because by the time you take off all your clothes you're out of the mood.

You know you're a Minnesotan if…

...in the winter you stand close to each other at bus stops to stay warm.

You know you're a Minnesotan if…

...you carry jumper cables in your car and figure it's not worth it to take them out of your trunk just for the summer.

You know you're a Minnesotan if…

...you have a hard time telling the sex of a person in the winter.

You know you're a Minnesotan if...
...you completely ignore snowstorms in **April**.

You know you're a Minnesotan if...
...you talk about the weather at least three times a day.

You know you're a Minnesotan if...
...you love hot days and cold nights.

You know you're a Minnesotan if...
...you don't zip your parka hood until it is really cold (-70 windchill).

ED FISCHER

<u>You know you're a Minnesotan if...</u>

...you have gotten frostbitten and sunburned in the same weekend.

<u>You know you're a Minnesotan if...</u>

...you miss the smell of burning leaves in the city.

<u>You know you're a Minnesotan if...</u>

...you're always surprised when you get a sunburn.

<u>You know you're a Minnesotan if...</u>

...you say "it's not the heat, it's the humidity" at least 50 times in a summer.

MINNESAUNA

You know you're a Minnesotan if...

...you can't leave the house until you know what the temperature is.

You know you're a Minnesotan if...

...at get-togethers the conversation is always about...

WINTER: Insulation
SPRING: Lawns
SUMMER: It's the humidity, not the heat
FALL: Insulation

You know you're a Minnesotan if...

...you consider Minnesota to be the coldest place in the universe...and you're proud of it!

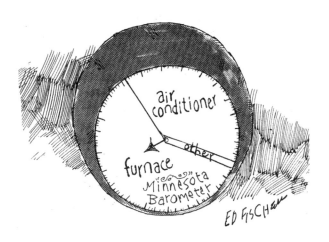

ED FISCHer

ETHNIC

You know you're a Minnesotan if…

...**Uff Da!** is an exclamation you use when something unexpected happens...like when the tree you cut down lands on your neighbor's roof.

You know you're a Minnesotan if…

...your dog goes 'wuff da.'

You know you're a Minnesotan if…

...you feel you have proven you are a tolerant human being and not a bigot, because you are Norwegian and you still go to a Swedish picnic.

You know you're a Minnesotan if…

...you go to church suppers, but 200 Norwegians in one place makes you edgy.

Welcome to
MINNESOTA
• 10,000 LAKES
• 100,000 PETERSONS

ED FISCHER

FISHING/HUNTING

You know you're a Minnesotan if...

...you feel bait shops are what life's all about.

You know you're a Minnesotan if...

...your boat is so powerful it can go around the lake in 30 seconds. Then you wonder what you'll do for the rest of the day.

You know you're a Minnesotan if...

...you think a woman's place is in the kitchen cleaning fish, but, then, had to think again.

You know you're a Minnesotan if...

...you consider the opening day of fishing to be a religious holiday.

You know you're a Minnesotan if...

...you've water skied and scared folks in a fishing boat.

You know you're a Minnesotan if...

...you were so desperate on a fishing trip you brought home 40 perch.

You know you're a Minnesotan if...

...the smell of dead fish whets your appetite.

You know you're a Minnesotan if...

...you can skin bullheads and hate it when people ask why.

You know you're a Minnesotan if...

...you've eaten a sandwich right after putting a worm on the hook.

You know you're a Minnesotan if…

…you get a little trigger happy when you're the only one without a deer.

You know you're a Minnesotan if…

…you sit in a duck blind when it's cold, damp and raining because that hot coffee tastes so darn good.

You know you're a Minnesotan if…

…you think you've helped the family food budget by bringing home a couple of ducks from a $800 hunting trip.

You know you're a Minnesotan if…

…a buddy falls from a tree after shooting a deer and you don't know who to save, the buddy or the deer.

SPORTS

You know you're a Minnesotan if...

...you see one deer on the highway there are likely more to follow. In the same way, if you see one cheesehead, chances are there are likely more to follow.

You know you're a Minnesotan if...

...your prayers have something to do with the Vikings.

You know you're a Minnesotan if...

...you think the Norwegian vikings were anything like the football team, they would have capsized, drowned, and would have never discovered America.

ED FISCHER

You know you're a Minnesotan if...

...you blamed the Twins season on La Nina.

You know you're a Minnesotan if...

...you now use the 'homer hankie' to cry at Twins games.

You know you're a Minnesotan if...

...you go to car races because you like the smell.

Minnesota face-off 2

ED FISCHER

'TOO HARD! TOO HARD!'

RELIGION

You know you're a Minnesotan if…

…you wonder a little why the pastor only looks at you when he preaches about sin.

You know you're a Minnesotan if…

…a prayer circle member you know swears that miracles happen because she prayed and prayed and her husband has stopped telling that awful dirty joke over and over.

You know you're a Minnesotan if…

…you had to stop going to polka mass because you bounced down to communion without the music.

You know you're a Minnesotan if…

…you were 'born again' at a polka mass.

ED FISCHER

You know you're a Minnesotan if...

...75% of the dishes at your church supper have those dried onions on top.

You know you're a Minnesotan if...

...you are sure all church basements are painted the same green for a reason.

You know you're a Minnesotan if...

...you had to talk to the minister because you've tried and tried and could not forgive Louise Swenson for playing that trump in bridge.

You know you're a Minnesotan if...

...you wondered a little why the reverend on his last visit put his hand on your head and prayed for twenty minutes.

You know you're a Minnesotan if...

...you looked for some reference in the Bible for coffee get-togethers.

HI-TEST coffee

ED FISCHER

WEIGHT

You know you're a Minnesotan if...

...you consider bowling to be an exercise program.

You know you're a Minnesotan if...

...you have figured out that you could spend a year at a spa in France for what you've spent over the years on exercise equipment.

You know you're a Minnesotan if...

...you sometimes think: so many cakes-so little time.

You know you're a Minnesotan if...

...you wish they didn't have so many good places to eat at the Mall where you're walking to lose weight.

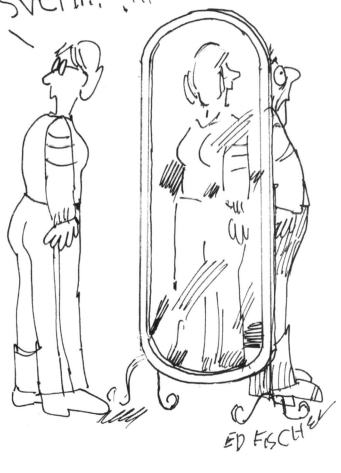

SOCIAL

You know you're a Minnesotan if...

...you were ashamed you only had one kind of cookie for unexpected company.

You know you're a Minnesotan if...

...you love to surprise dinner guests by telling them they've just eaten squirrel and Rocky Mountain oysters.

You know you're a Minnesotan if...

...the only time you feel comfortable talking about sex is when you're telling an Ole and Lena joke.

You know you're a Minnesotan if...

...you won't let visitors leave until all the sweet rolls are gone.

Mildred—maybe Harry doesn't want another of your rolls...

ED FISCHER

You know you're a Minnesotan if...

...you clean your house because the cleaning lady is coming.

You know you're a Minnesotan if...

...you know at least one family that has a beautifully decorated room that nobody can go into.

You know you're a Minnesotan if...

...the car in front of you has been sitting at a green light for five minutes and you're thinking about honking the horn.

You know you're a Minnesotan if...

...you feed people without asking them if they're hungry.

You know you're a Minnesotan if...

...you honk the car horn only if you're driving away from a relative's house.

You know you're a Minnesotan if…

…you consider it bad manners to make a face when someone lets one loose in the elevator.

You know you're a Minnesotan if…

…you consider it good manners to give every visitor a beer even if they didn't ask for it.

You know you're a Minnesotan if…

…you go for a fish fry every Friday night but you hate to go to a fish fry every Friday night.

You know you're a Minnesotan if…

…you ask if anyone would like the last hotdog after you've taken a big bite out of it.

You know you're a Minnesotan if…

…you consider bingo to be a cultural event.

ON THE ROAD

…you had a game that you played on Sunday drives in the country to see who could identify the farm smells.

…you have experienced cross country skiing, church outside under the tall pines, and wild rice pancakes for breakfast.

…you know of a town with 30 people and 3 bars.

You know you're a Minnesotan if…

…when you have to turn on your car lights in a pothole.

You know you're a Minnesotan if…

…you shopped at the Mall of America once, but won't go back because it doesn't have a Hardware Hank.

You know you're a Minnesotan if…

…you go to relax at your cabin up north partly to relieve tension built up from the traffic.

MISCELLANEOUS

You know you're a Minnesotan if…

...you feel chopping wood for heating the house would save a lot of money on your fuel bill and can't understand why your wife won't do it.

You know you're a Minnesotan if…

...you went to a farm auction once and have no idea what you're going to do with the corn picker you bought.

You know you're a Minnesotan if…

...you put your Target gift in a Daytons box.

You know you're a Minnesotan if…

...you have fond memories of the Hamms' Bear.

You know you're a Minnesotan if…

…you pronounce 'roof' like a Saint Bernard.

You know you're a Minnesotan if…

…you sometimes wonder why machinery hill at the State Fair is not on a hill.

You know you're a Minnesotan if…

…you had your house blessed but that peculiar smell is still there.

You know you're a Minnesotan if…

…you call someone on the phone and ask 'are you sleeping?'

You know you're a Minnesotan if…

…you spend hundreds of dollars at casinos, but go because the food is cheap.

<u>You know you're a Minnesotan if…</u>

…you wear a Harvard sweatshirt but you've never been out of the state of Minnesota.

<u>You know you're a Minnesotan if…</u>

…you can't quite remember that dirty joke about Betty Crocker, the Pillsbury Dough Boy, and the Hamburger Helper hand.

<u>You know you're a Minnesotan if…</u>

…you can identify a Northeast Minneapolis accent.

<u>You know you're a Minnesotan if…</u>

…you know SPAM is what we did to the rest of the world for making fun of Minnesota.

Northlands Nudist Colony
MEDICAL ALERT

DO NOT attempt to play the accordian naked!

ED FISCHER

You know you're a Minnesotan if…

…you drive a tractor but can't get a drivers license for at least another eight years.

You know you're a Minnesotan if…

…the most exciting thing in your life is watching the guy at the county fair make an eagle out of a tree stump with a chainsaw.

You know you're a Minnesotan if…

…your Governor's idea of a veto is a body slam.

You know you're a Minnesotan if…

…you know if you survive Minnesota…the rest of the world is a piece of cake.

You know you're a Minnesotan if…

…you go to Arizona to get a tan…in August.

Minnesota Drivers Training

repeat after me… I pledge to adjust my mirror…fasten my seat belt and never, never slow down for a pedestrian…

ED FISCHER

You know you're a Minnesotan if...

...you think seed catalogs are 'heavy reading.'

You know you're a Minnesotan if...

...you think it's fun that Minnesota is probably the only state with an artist that paints with goose doo doo.

You know you're a Minnesotan if...

...you have a picture of a cardinal on your mailbox.

You know you're a Minnesotan if...

...your idea of a good business deal is getting a good price at a garage sale.

You know you're a Minnesotan if...

...you sent public radio money to shut them up at fund raising time.

MAIL

SEED CATALOGS

ED FISCHER

You know you're a Minnesotan if...

...as a teen you showed your affection to someone special by filling her tree with toilet paper.

You know you're a Minnesotan if...

...your most prized possession is a tool.

You know you're a Minnesotan if...

...you have 200 tools, but haven't used 198 of them in 2 years.

You know you're a Minnesotan if...

...you use the expression "I'm not going there," or "no problem" at least once every 15 minutes.

You know you're a Minnesotan if...

...the discussion at the coffee shop is about subjects like: Someday will there be a 'Viagra Anonymous?'

You know you're a Minnesotan if...

...you have 21 ways to fix anything.

You know you're a Minnesotan if...

...you consider mowing grass when you can't see the plastic deer.

Minnesota Valentine

you're not too shabby

ED FISCHER

<u>You know you're a Minnesotan if...</u>

...your answer to the question "what do you grow in Minnesota?" is, "older and older."

<u>You know you're a Minnesotan if...</u>

...you've learned never to slap a boyfriend who chews 'snoose.'

<u>You know you're a Minnesotan if...</u>

...it's the last time you'll go tubing down the river sober.

<u>You know you're a Minnesotan if...</u>

...a night out is taking your significant other to Sears and for an Orange Julius.

ED FISCHER

You know you're a Minnesotan if...

...you celebrate your 40th birthday and wonder 'what the hell am I doing here!?.'

You know you're a Minnesotan if...

...you've been attacked by a rooster.

You know you're a Minnesotan if...

...your idea of a good time is sitting in an unbelievably hot sauna.

You know you're a Minnesotan if...

...your idea of a great time is sitting in an unbelievably hot sauna with someone whipping you with a twig.

You know you're a Minnesotan if...

...your idea of ecstasy is running out of a sauna naked and rolling in the snow after being whipped with a twig in an unbelievably hot sauna.

minnesota TEST

Name the plan most
Minnesota towns use
to rid the streets
of huge amounts
of snow

Answer:

spring

FAMILY

You know you're a Minnesotan if…

...you have a mother who says 'if you get killed, don't come running to me.'

You know you're a Minnesotan if…

...your mother worries that keeping your last name when getting married may be interpreted by some that you are not married.

You know you're a Minnesotan if…

...you feel you're in touchy areas with some relatives if you talk about anything other than the weather or sports...and you're not too sure about sports.

You know you're a Minnesotan if…

...you couldn't take your wife to the hospital until after the news and weather.

ED FISCHER

Sorry - you can't leave the store until you buy more veggies...

MOM'S HEALTH FOOD SHOP

You know you're a Minnesotan if...

...you have at least one relative who slept with the window open in the winter...and she died young.

You know you're a Minnesotan if...

...when you are talking about wild turkeys, you're usually referring to your inlaws.

You know you're a Minnesotan if...

...you thought things were pretty congenial at the family get-together until they started to play whist.

You know you're a Minnesotan if...

...you had a mom who ironed and neatly folded your underwear.

Minnesota Mom's "V" chip

KIDS: IF YOU WATCH THIS SHOW, YOU'LL GO BLIND

ED FISCHER

ENVIRONMENT

You know you're a Minnesotan if...

...you never carry a compass because there are other ways to find your way around and you have never been lost for more than a couple of days.

You know you're a Minnesotan if...

...you always check for ticks after a walk in the woods – but, of course can't check on a two-week vacation in the boundary waters.

You know you're a Minnesotan if...

...you think the North Shore is just like the French Riviera except there's no sun to speak of, the water is too cold to swim in, and the only food that is close to exotic is the smoked carp.

You know you're a Minnesotan if…

…there's a story you've kept to yourself about the time you were sitting in an outhouse doing a number two when a bat suddenly went crazy in the building.

You know you're a Minnesotan if…

…you have experienced a brisk fall morning walk in the leaves and came home to a fire in the fireplace, bacon, eggs, and homemade bread.

You know you're a Minnesotan if…

…roughing it is doing without a TV at a fancy resort up north.

You know you're a Minnesotan if…

…camping out was great, except for the mosquitoes, stifling steamy weather, and that raccoon that ran away with your car keys.

You know you're a Minnesotan if…

…you find it harder to go to the lake swimming once you've whizzed in the water because it occurs to you that everyone else may be doing it too.

You know you're a Minnesotan if…

…you hate it when you go swimming in a lake and you swallow that green stuff with strange looking bugs.

You know you're a Minnesotan if…

…you always go to the State Mosquito Festival – held after every rain.

You know you're a Minnesotan if…

…you once killed a mosquito you almost took to the taxidermist.

You know you're a Minnesotan if…

…you have used pepper spray to stun mosquitoes.

ED FISCHER

OPINIONS

You know you're a Minnesotan if...

...you think the Jolly Green Giant wouldn't be so jolly if he got a good whiff of the canning operation in Le Sueur.

You know you're a Minnesotan if...

...you think it's a good idea that fat veterans are in the parade getting some exercise.

You know you're a Minnesotan if...

...you don't mind high state taxes because of the 'quality of life.'

You know you're a Minnesotan if...

...you think Rocky and Bullwinkle would make better representatives in Saint Paul than the bozos we have there now.

You know you're a Minnesotan if...

...you believe 10 minutes in a sauna cures anything.

You know you're a Minnesotan if...

...you feel Jon Grunseth was the only exciting thing to ever happen in Minnesotan politics.

You know you're a Minnesotan if…

...you consider yourself a naturalist when you walk in the woods because you know a weed when you see one.

You know you're a Minnesotan if…

...you attribute Minnesotan longevity to clean living, hard work and Garrison Keillor.

You know you're a Minnesotan if…

...you don't like Texas but you don't know why.

You know you're a Minnesotan if…

...you are not surprised at anything you hear about California.

You know you're a Minnesotan if…

...your idea of great landscaping is three statues of deer and that wooden woman bending over to pick flowers.

You know you're a Minnesotan if…

...you feel Arizona is for sissies.

You know you're a Minnesotan if…

...you think any home in Minnesota without a basement is unfinished.

<u>You know you're a Minnesotan if…</u>

…you consider **Myron Floren** to be the greatest accordion player of all time. But then he's the only accordion player you know.

<u>You know you're a Minnesotan if…</u>

…you think that it's not too surprising that there are more bars in Minnesota than there are schools.